The Official
<u>IRS Tax Guide</u>
to Auditing Horse Activities

THE RUSSELL MEERDINK COMPANY, LTD.
NEENAH, WI 54956

Disclaimer

The purpose of this book is to serve as a guideline to help taxpayers involved in horse activities gain a deeper understanding of what is needed to keep their horse business in compliance with IRS regulations, and what to expect if audited. It is not meant to cover all aspects of tax rules governing horse activities and all situations that may arise, nor does it replace the assistance of a tax professional.

The publisher is not engaged in rendering tax or legal services. The publisher does not make any recommendations, warranties or representations, express or implied, of this book's content, and assumes no liability in regard to the use of the information within this publication.

ISBN 0-929346-70-X

Published by

The Russell Meerdink Company, Ltd.
1555 South Park Avenue
Neenah, WI 54956
(920) 725-0955 Worldwide • (800) 635-6499 U.S. & Canada
www.horseinfo.com

Printed in the United States of America

Introduction

Each year horse owners face the potential of a tax audit of their horse operations by the Internal Revenue Service.

The IRS may seek to disallow what the horse owner considers legitimate operating expenses on the basis that the horse operation is a hobby for the taxpayer and not a real "for-profit" business operation.

The IRS agents have at their disposal a concise guide for determining the criteria a horse operation must meet to be considered a legitimate business under the IRS Code. Unfortunately, most horse owners do not have access to the same information as the agent who will investigate their operations.

IRS auditors operate under the premise that the horse operation is a hobby and not a legitimate for-profit business. They will seek to disallow the operation based on a series of pointed questions, unique issues, tax laws and court cases. By arming themselves with the same information as the IRS auditor, horse owners can put their operations in compliance with the tax code and protect their interests.

The IRS arms its agents with fact-gathering guides through the Market Segment Specialization Program. There are audit guides for just about every type of business — from bail bondsmen to taxi cabs. The Audit Techniques Guide on IRC section 183 Farm Hobby Losses has been developed to provide a tool to revenue agents and tax auditors pursuing the application of section 183 to prove that the horse operation in question is not engaged in a "for-profit" activity.

This book is the actual IRS Audit Guide for horse operations.

This page left intentionally blank.

IRC section 183: Farm Hobby Losses
With Cattle Operations and Horse Activities

Table of Contents

Market Segement Specialization Program

IRC Section 183: Farm Hobby Losses with Cattle Operations and Horse Activities

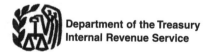 Department of the Treasury
Internal Revenue Service

Training 3123-015 (3-01)
TPDS No. 86796N

This page left intentionally blank.

Introduction

STATEMENT OF PURPOSE

The Market Segment Specialization Program (MSSP) Audit Techniques Guide (ATG) on IRC section 183 Farm Hobby Losses has been developed to provide guidance to Revenue Agents and Tax Auditors in pursuing the application of IRC section 183 with respect to horse activities and cattle operations.

Historically, IRC section 183 has been a difficult issue to pursue. The development of the issue is a fact-gathering initiative. The application of IRC section 183 is based upon the examiner's understanding of the taxpayer's industry as well as the taxpayer's mode of operation within that industry. IRC section 183 and the accompanying Treasury Regulations do not provide absolute definition, but serve to provide guidance in formulating the facts into a conclusion.

Hazards of litigation have also been a deterrent toward the pursuit of IRC section 183. As a result, examiners have been reluctant to allocate exam time. This ATG will help to further develop the weaker areas within these cases and reduce the hazards of litigation.

While IRC section 183 has been referred as the Hobby Loss section of the Internal Revenue Code, examiners should refrain from using such terminology. The actual language of the Code refers to "Activities Not Engaged in for Profit." Some taxpayers resist this "hobby" terminology and the implications therein. For whatever reason taxpayers have engaged in these activities, albeit for the pleasure of a hobby or the tax benefits derived, these activities were not engaged in for the sake of deriving a profit.

The examiner should use this guide during all phases of an examination where the provisions of IRC section 183 may be applicable. The purpose of the ATG is to:

• Provide background about the market segment.
• Identify frequent and/or unique issues.
• Provide examination techniques.
• Discuss use of applicable law and court cases.

This guide is not designed to be all-inclusive.

OBJECTIVES

The use of this audit techniques guide will enable the examiner to:

1. Identify and develop issues specific to the market segment.
2. Conduct an examination consistent with other market segment examinations throughout the Service.

Chapter 1

Market Segment Definition and Overview

PURPOSE

This chapter describes horse activities and cattle operations in an overview format. Special emphasis will focus on the application of IRC section 183 to each market segment. This provides the examiner with necessary background information to have a working knowledge of the market segment.

The following text provides the examiner with a brief overview of both cattle operations and horse activities.

DEFINITION

A brief description of the business types covered in this chapter will be discussed. While any activity engaged by the taxpayer could potentially fall under the provisions of IRC section 183, the focus of this ATG is horse activities and cattle operations. Current trends indicate that these two activities, due to their nature, contain certain opportunities for taxpayer abuse. Examiners need to gain an understanding of these activities to make a determination whether the provisions of IRC section 183 will apply to their taxpayer.

BACKGROUND

The historical perspective of each market segment are reviewed.

Many of the taxpayers who potentially fall under the provisions of IRC section 183 with respect to horse and cattle activities have been involved in such activities during their youth. These taxpayers have grown up on farms or had close relatives who operated farms. Other taxpayers had unfulfilled childhood aspirations to be involved with such activities, but circumstances prevented participation. As adults, these taxpayers have achieved the financial wherewithal which permits participation.

The taxpayers who have had prior experience in these activities find peace and solace in returning to this lifestyle. These taxpayers have affection for the horses as well as the cattle. The taxpayers find pleasure and satisfaction from watching their herds and baby animals grazing in the pastures. Examiners will frequently find retirement homes nestled on the land set aside for the activity.

Horse activities provide a competitive outlet for some taxpayers. For example, some taxpayers have been quoted as saying that cutting horse competitions provide stress relief from the chaos in the corporate world.

Some taxpayers have found that agricultural status will reduce the property taxes on their land. Small numbers of cattle have been maintained on large parcels of land in order to qualify for this agricultural status. In such situations, the cattle activity was not engaged in for profit, but rather for the purpose of reducing property taxes. In other words, taxpayers have engaged in horse and cattle activities to reduce taxable income for Federal income tax purposes and to reduce property taxes. The property tax benefit is more attractive with land parcels that are larger than a few acres.

CURRENT STATUS

This section includes current information about horse activities and cattle operations. Discussion includes current trends, unique business practices, and forms of operation.

Horse Activities

Between the two activities of horses and cattle, horse activities more readily lend to the provisions of IRC section 183. Many publications have been written that direct taxpayers to use horse activities as a means to incur tax losses. These articles teach the taxpayer how to skirt the provisions of IRC section 183. Thus, the phrase "horse shelter" has evolved. If any taxpayers have followed this lead, then these taxpayers have entered the activity without a profit motivation; however, no taxpayer would ever confess this reason for entering an activity.

Horse activities encompass a broad span of activities for which a taxpayer may participate. A taxpayer can participate in one activity exclusively or in a combination of the activities. Some of the activities, when combined together, may or may not generate expenses that are ordinary and necessary. For example, Showing Expense would not be an ordinary and necessary expense to Gross Receipts derived from horse boarding. This concept will be discussed in further detail later in the text.

Horses are like athletes. They can be trained to perform events or to work certain jobs. Therefore, some horses will be frequently referred to as performance horses or working horses. Performance horses may be further distinguished by the event for which they have been specially trained. Such references would include, but are not limited to, roping, cutting, reining, and so forth.

At times, horses are referenced by the inherent qualities possessed by virtue of their bloodlines. Hence, a horse may be called "Halter bred" if his or her bloodlines come from a lineage strong in Halter horses.

Halter horses are not considered Performance horses. Halter horses are defined by their muscular build. They are judged for their conformation to their breed characteristics and standards. Halter horses are not ridden in competition. Instead, halter horses are shown with the exhibitor leading the horse from the ground.

Horses are further distinguished by breeds. For example, there are Appaloosas, Arabians, Palominos, Morgans, Saddlebreds, National Show Horses, Tennessee Walkers, Thoroughbreds, Quarter Horses, Warmbloods, Paints, Pintos, draft horses, Andalusians, Peruvian Paso, Miniatures, and ponies. (This is not an all-inclusive list). Each breed is known for significant attributes which distinguishes that breed from other breeds; however, more than one breed may be used to perform certain events. For example, both Thoroughbreds and Quarter Horses may be used for racing. While Thoroughbreds are generally more proficient for racing by virtue of genetic breeding, Quarter Horses have also proven themselves to be successful on quarter-mile tracks.

Each horse breed has its own breed association. These associations govern the registrations of their horses, set forth rules and regulations governing competitions, and oversee their Code of Ethics or Conduct. Any breeders who violate the guidelines may be suspended from the breed association for certain infractions.

Examiners should determine which breed association governs the taxpayer. The examiner can gain a wealth of information from these breed associations such as the number of horses registered by the taxpayer in a given year, any rules infractions or violations, or points earned in competitions. The examiner will most likely need to use a summons to gather information specific to a taxpayer. However, general information regarding the breed and the breed association is provided for free. A telephone call from the examiner will be sufficient in order to receive such promotional materials. Many times this information is also published in the respective breed journals. The examiner may be able to gather breed association information from the Internet in districts where access is available. This information can be used to paint a picture of the taxpayer's situation and help determine the applicability of IRC section 183.

Horse Training

Training Expense can be either an ordinary and necessary expense or a nondeductible, personal expense.

A horse must be trained to make it useful by people. The training process can be an ongoing process with varying stages, depending upon the use and intended purpose of the horse.

In theory, a horse should have a higher market value upon successful completion of its training; however, a weanling with highly desirable bloodlines and genetics may sell at a high market price without any training at all.

After horses have been broke to ride with a saddle, they may receive additional specialized training to learn performance events such as cutting or reining.

Depending upon the taxpayer's expertise and background, the taxpayer may choose to train his or her own horses. Most frequently, trainers are hired to train the horses for the taxpayer. This process is sometimes referred to as "putting time on the horse." Training is incurred in 30-day increments. Time spent on specialized training would be contingent upon the needs and learning capacity of the individual horse.

The cost for training includes the trainer's time, board, and care while the horse is at the trainer's facility.

Examiners should determine what local trainers generally charge in their respective districts. Examiners should consider profit motivation in situations whereby significant training fees are expended with little or no gross receipts derived from the activity. Examiners should determine why the horses are being trained. Are the horses being held primarily for resale? Are the horses to be used in competitions with prize money to be earned? Do the gross receipts derived, if any, justify the expenses incurred to train the horses?

When training fees exceed gross receipts or the reasonable expectation of gross receipts, the examiner needs to consider the profit motivation of the taxpayer.

Boarding

Boarding horses can be a source of revenue or a deductible expense under IRC section 162. In certain situations, boarding may be a personal, nondeductible expense.

Taxpayers can derive substantial income from boarding horses. Examiners need to determine standard boarding rates in their respective districts. Boarding fees are set according to services provided for the boarders. The most common boarding plans include full care, partial care, and self care. Examiners need to determine which type of plan that the taxpayer is utilizing.

Full care boarding generally provides that the stable performs all basic care of the horse. This care includes feeding twice daily, cleaning the stall, and turning the horse out for exercise. The stable also supplies the feed and hay for the horse. Additional fees may be charged to the boarders for worming and farrier visits, if provided by the stable. Full care boarding is the most expensive of the three boarding plans.

Partial care boarding generally provides that the stable feeds the horse, but the owner is responsible for all other care needs such as cleaning the stalls. The examiner should review the boarding agreement to define the responsibilities of each party. Partial care boarding is less expensive than full care boarding.

Self-care boarding generally provides that the stable supplies a stall for the horse and the owner is responsible for all remaining care of the horse. The owner must feed the horse and clean the stall. The owner must also provide their own feed and hay. Since the stable only provides stalls and no other services, this is the least expensive method of boarding for the owner.

The examiner's understanding of the boarding arrangements will prove significant as the examiner determines the nature of the expense as well as the level of the taxpayer's participation.

Boarding horses can be an ordinary and necessary expense under the provisions of IRC section 162 depending upon the horse activity. However, boarding expenses can also be personal in nature. Boarding expenses can also be indicative of a passive activity. Examiners need to develop the facts of the situation to determine the proper tax treatment of these expenses.

Boarding expenditures can be incurred for a variety of situations. Examiners should be alert for situations where the taxpayer boards the horse and acts as an absentee owner. The examiner needs to consider the taxpayer's business intentions for owning the horse.

Horse Competitions

Horse competitions can be an important part of raising horses. These competitions provide a tool for measuring the performance ability of each horse. A horse that has earned many points is more marketable than a horse that has earned fewer points or none at all.

Horse competitions can provide revenue for the owner; however, not everyone can be the winner. Show prizes won may not cover the costs incurred to win the prizes. Entry fees will vary depending upon the show and the status of the show.

In addition to entry fees, stalls may be rented depending upon the length of the show. Desirable stall locations frequently command a higher stall rent. In other words, stalls located with easiest access to the show arena may rent for a higher fee.

Horse competitions can be useful for proving the merits of a horse; however, examiners should be alert for hobby potential. When a taxpayer consistently incurs significant show-related expenditures in conjunction with the showing activity, and the showing activity does not generate significant prize earnings or sale of horses, the examiner should consider the profit motivation of that taxpayer. Since some competitions award trophies and rosettes instead of cash prizes or points, examiners should determine specifically what the taxpayer is gaining from the showing activity.

Examiners should determine the specific classes in which the taxpayer participates. Examiners should also gain an understanding of the rules governing these classes because some classes evaluate the horse while other classes evaluate the rider. In the instances where the taxpayer has a significant amount of show fees deducted on the tax return, the examiner would find it worthwhile to determine the composition of these show fees. If the taxpayer participates in a significant number of classes whereby the taxpayer (rider) is evaluated instead of the horse, the examiner should consider the taxpayer's motivation for such participation. Regardless of class participation, significant show fees in relation to minimal show prizes could be indicative of a hobby motivation.

Other Expenses

Horse activities have other expenditures in relation to the activity. The examiner needs to evaluate each expenditure as it pertains to the taxpayer's situation and determine the deductibility under IRC section 162. After evaluating the whole set of facts and circumstances, the examiner needs to determine if the taxpayer is engaged in the activity with the intention of deriving an overall profit from the activity under the provisions of IRC section 183. The following expenditures are discussed to develop an understanding of the expenditure and how it applies to the individual taxpayer.

Any of the following expenses can be ordinary and necessary under IRC section 162 in the instances where the taxpayer has engaged in the activity for profit. However, if the examiner deems the activity not to be engaged in for profit, then the expense would be limited in accordance with IRC section 183. The limitations will be discussed in detail later in the text.

FEED EXPENSE is a common, self-explanatory expenditure. In the instances where the taxpayer has always boarded his or her horses, the tax return may not reflect any feed expense. The boarding expense would include the cost of feed for the horses in board. Examiners should be alert for feed expenditures for animals that are not integral to the operations of the activity. For example, expenses for the family's toy poodle may be contained and deducted within the feed expense. (Such personal expenses may be scattered throughout the other expenses as well).

INSURANCE EXPENSE can be an ordinary and necessary expense for the activity. The examiner should review the policies to determine the type of coverage and the asset protected by the coverage. The examiner should be alert for personal, nondeductible items. Horse insurance companies provide a variety of coverage, such theft, mortality, medical, liability, and loss of use, to name a few. Loss of use coverage is commonly obtained for horses that are utilized for specific purposes or "use". If the horse becomes unusable for that specific use because of injury, then the owner is compensated for the loss of use of that horse.

Insurance expense can be an indication that the taxpayer is trying to protect his investment. The examiner should weigh all facts and circumstances. The examiner should not conclude that an activity is engaged in for profit based solely upon the presence of insurance coverage.

Horse insurance companies state that policies are purchased by a variety of horse owners for a variety of reasons. Backyard ponies may be insured for a minimal amount if the owner does not have the financial wherewithal to readily replace the animal. Other wealthy horse owners may weigh the risk of loss against the need for insurance coverage. The owners may decide to forego coverage and elect to buy another horse should actual loss occur. For these owners, the replacement cost is insignificant. Nonetheless, the examiner should decide if the absence of insurance shows a lack of business prudence.

MARE CARE EXPENSE is generally incurred during the gestation cycle of the mare's pregnancy. The expense can include breeding the mare and providing postpartum foal care as well. The mare will often be sent to a special mare care facility, breeding facility, or mare motel. The examiner should consider the taxpayer's level of participation with respect to the activity in the instances of this expense coupled with other expenditures indicative of passive participation (such as boarding).

BREEDING FEES EXPENSE includes stud fees and any related veterinary costs. Booking fees would be paid to ensure a reservation for the mare to breed with the stud. Many stud owners limit the number of mares during the breeding season. The show record and progeny record of the mare may also be a criterion because the stud owners want their studs bred to top quality mares. These owners believe that quality offspring result from quality pairings. They do not want substandard-quality offspring produced with their stud's name in the pedigree. Not all stud owners hold to these criteria for varying reasons. For example, owners of unproven studs or studs with limited showings might not be particular about the mare's record. (An unproven stud is generally young and does not have offspring produced to date to measure his abilities).

Horses may be bred using artificial insemination or naturally (live cover). The method of live cover can subject either horse (mare or stud) to injuries related to the process, such as biting or kicking. Owners may not wish to subject valuable horses to such potential injuries and elect to use artificial insemination. In general, artificial insemination is the more expensive method. The taxpayer's choice of method is a matter of preference and not an indication of profit motive.

PRACTICE CATTLE EXPENSE pertains to cattle used as a practice aid for cutting horses. Practice cattle need to be exchanged periodically so that the cutting horses are using "fresh" cattle. Practice cattle can be rented at cutting horse competitions. In such instances, practice cattle would be an expense to the taxpayer. Sometimes, the taxpayer may wish to maintain his or her own practice cattle at his or her horse facility. In such instances, the taxpayer will purchase cattle and use them for a period of time. After the cattle are no longer "fresh", he or she will sell them at a sale barn and purchase new cattle.

The examiner should determine the exact nature of the practice cattle. The taxpayer may fail to report the income derived from the sale of practice cattle maintained on his or her cutting horse facility.

Cattle Operations

There are several methods for operating cattle activities. While these methods have similarities, there are also differences.

Cattle operations have developed the use of various data to monitor productivity of the cattle and the profitability of the cattle operation. As a result, many terms and definitions have evolved. The glossary at the end of this guide explains some of these terms. The examiner may also contact the local County Agricultural Extension Agent for additional information.

The biggest distinguishing factor among cattle operations lies within the registration of the herd. A taxpayer may choose to register his or her herd with a recognized breed association. This choice mandates that the taxpayer adheres to policies set forth by the governing breed association. These policies are designed to preserve the purity and integrity of the breed. The breed association also requires that records be maintained to track the productivity of every registered animal.

Taxpayers may choose not to raise registered purebred cattle. Depending upon regional phraseology, an unregistered herd may be referred to as a **COMMERCIAL HERD**. While such a choice relieves the taxpayer from the government of a breed association, the taxpayer still needs to maintain a recordkeeping system that tracks the efficiency of the cattle operation.

Types of Cattle Operations

Cattle operations can be further defined by the end product. Cattle operations may produce one or a combination of products for sale.

COW-CALF OPERATIONS are comprised of a herd of cows that produce an annual calf crop. These calves are sold after they are weaned from their mothers. The taxpayer has several options for marketing these calves.

Calves may be sold as **FEEDER CALVES**. The buyers may be feedlots, who buy weaned calves and feed these calves until slaughter weight. The taxpayer may raise the feeder calves and sell them to a packer when slaughter weight has been achieved.

Calves may be sold as BREEDING STOCK, registered or commercial, to other breeders. The taxpayer may retain some of his or her heifer calves for **REPLACEMENT HEIFERS** in his or her own breeding program. Any calves sold for breeding stock may be heifers, bulls, or both.

Live calves are not the only products from cow-calf operations. Modern medical technology has enabled cattlemen to sell semen from prized bulls. **EMBRYOS** from prized genetics may also be sold. **SEMEN SALES** require that the taxpayer issue breeding certificates. The examiner could verify income from semen sales through these breeding certificates.

The taxpayer will have incidental income from the sale of **CULL CATTLE** at the local sale barn. Culls may be sold singly or in small group. The examiner should be alert for cull sales because these smaller sales are frequently overlooked in calculating income from the activity. Checks received from the sale barn may be cashed and not deposited into the bank account.

The examiner needs to establish the taxpayer's method of operation with respect to the cattle activity, or the horse activity, during the Initial Interview.

Books and Records

Horse activities and cattle operations have unique recordkeeping systems. Completeness of these books and records should be considered while the examiner develops Factor One, Manner in Which the Taxpayer Carries on the Activity.

Books and Records for Horse Activities

Recordkeeping for horses should be complete and useful so the taxpayer can make informed business decisions about the activity. Horse records are similar to cattle operations except horsemen do not concern themselves with any weightrelated data. Horsemen should focus on the production and performance of each horse and any resulting offspring of each horse. Superior production and performance will impact the profitability of the activity.

Complete and accurate contemporaneous field records will ensure accurate pedigrees for the certificates of registrations. This is a requirement for compliance with any governing breed association.

The examiner should be aware that many breed associations offer online Internet access to members that enable access to show winnings, pedigrees, and other data maintained by the association. The examiner should discern whether the taxpayer maintains any separate records or if the taxpayer relies upon association records.

Books and Records for Beef Cattle Operations

The examiner should be alert that some taxpayers may not maintain the contemporaneous records necessary to satisfy the requirements of the breed association. Some of the data may be "plugged." Contemporaneous records would include some type of field book that is carried out to the pasture. The data would be transferred from the field book to a permanent record.

Contemporaneous records lend to the reliability of the herd's production records. Unreliable records will not assist the taxpayer in making informed business decisions about the cattle operation. The examiner should review the recordkeeping process and make comments regarding completeness. The taxpayer's use of incomplete records could indicate a lack of profit motive.

The taxpayer may choose not to register his or her herd with a recognized breed association. While recordkeeping burden has been reduced, the taxpayer should still maintain meaningful production records in order to track production and control profitability through informed business decisions.

Meaningful production records will work much like a cost accounting system. Each cow, bull, and steer is a unit of production. The bulls and cows will produce calves. The steers will produce beef carcasses. The efficiency of each producer should be monitored.

Example 1

A cow-calf operation would monitor birth date (calving date), sex of the offspring, birth weights, weaning weights, and yearling weights for each calf produced. The production records may also show data regarding the cow's milk production for the calf.

Example 2

A feeder steer operation would monitor type of feed, percentage of feed ingredients, beginning weight, daily rate of gain (weight), weight per day of age, slaughter weight, and USDA yield grade of carcass.

Factor One addresses the manner in which the taxpayer carries on the activity. While the completeness of the taxpayer's records may indicate a profit motive, the examiner must evaluate the taxpayer's operation from the perspective of all nine relevant factors.

FUTURE OUTLOOK

Several publications have promoted the use of horse activities as a means to lower taxable income. Thus, the term "horse shelter" has been coined. These publications have skirted the provisions of IRC section 183. Cattle operations have also enabled taxpayers to lower their taxable income. These "shelters" have been attractive because the Internal Revenue Service has not aggressively pursued this issue in times past for various reasons. United States Tax Court cases have ruled both ways and encouraged the taxpayer's engagement of such activities.

In general, taxpayers in higher income tax brackets will benefit from the engagement of these activities. Improved case development will further the Government's success in litigating this issue and reduce the taxpayer's abuse of this Internal Revenue Code section.

RESOURCES

There are additional IRS resources available to the examiner. Resources include:

• Technical Advisors
• Project Coordinator
• District Market Segment Specialization Program Coordinator
• General Livestock Audit Technique Guide
• Farmer's Tax Guide, IRS Publication

Page left intentionally blank.

Chapter 2

Issues

PURPOSE

This chapter discusses specific issues applicable to horse activities and cattle operations. These issues are limited to those which are frequent or unique to the horse and cattle market segments.

Frequent issues occur regularly in the market segment. For example, showing horses and cattle, without regard for costs versus benefit, is encountered frequently.

Unique issues are found only within the market segment. For example, the history of losses issue is unique to the IRC section 183 cases.

ISSUES

Issues specific to each market segment will be discussed. This discussion will include the following points:

• Overview of the issue
• Automatic adjustments apparent on the face of the return (for example, depreciation methods used for breeding stock and farm equipment)
• Frequency
• Discussion of each of the nine relevant factors.

PRE-EXAMINATION ANALYSIS

The examiner needs to develop the ability to inspect a tax return and determine the potential for that taxpayer's activity to fall under the provisions of IRC section 183.

REVIEW OF TAX RETURN

Examiners need to consider a number of aspects about the tax return. Inspection of the tax return needs to include certain relevant factors as contained in the Treasury Regulations for IRC section 183. The nine relevant factors of Treasury Regulation section 1.183-2(b) are discussed later in the text.

Observe whether the activity has any gross income. In many instances, there will be little or no gross income. Consider the source of the income. This information may be contained on a separate statement within the tax return. The source may not be directly related to the activity as specified on the Schedule. In order to legitimize the activity as a business, or make it appear as an activity engaged in for profit, a taxpayer may place income from wholly unrelated sources to offset the large expenses for the activity.

A separate statement may indicate "Show Prizes" as an income source. Another separate statement may explain "Other Expenses" to include a significant amount of show expenses that far exceed the income derived from "Show Prizes." This should alert the examiner to a strong indication that a hobby may be present. Consider why the taxpayer's costs (show expenses) of the activity have exceeded the benefits (prizes or sales).

The examiner will need to secure the original returns for each year that the taxpayer has conducted the activity in the event that District Counsel litigates the case in United States Tax Court.

REPORTING ON SCHEDULE C OR SCHEDULE F

Taxpayers have been reporting cattle operations and horse activities on Schedules F as well as Schedules C. The taxpayer's choice to utilize Schedule C or Schedule F is not a determinative consideration in the application of IRC section 183. Taxpayers have their own justification for using either Schedule C or F. The use of either Schedule is acceptable and has no bearing in proving whether an activity is engaged in for profit. Classifiers and examiners should be alert that the use of Schedule C could potentially disguise the nature of a farming activity that would be subject to the provisions of IRC section 183.

HISTORY OF LOSSES

The examiner needs to obtain information regarding the taxpayer's history of the activity under consideration. During the pre-examination analysis, the examiner could gain such information from a MACS 3-year printout or from Information Data Retrieval System (IDRS). The examiner should defer to whichever method is most readily available and recommended in the examiner's district.

The examiner needs to review the history and determine if the activity is generating any profits in any years at all. If the taxpayer has received any profits on an occasional basis, the examiner should determine if the overall history of losses exceeds the occasional profits.

IRC section 183(d) addresses the presumption that if an activity's gross income exceeds attributable deductions for 3 or more of the taxable years in a period of 5 consecutive taxable years, then the activity is presumed to be engaged in for profit, regardless of whether the activity is engaged in for profit. For the purpose of this text, cattle operations fall under this presumption. Activities that pertain to the breeding, training, or showing of horses should observe a profit in 2 or more of the taxable years in a period of 7 consecutive taxable years.

Aside from the presumption stated in IRC section 183(d), Treasury Regulation section 1.183-2(b)(6) addresses the taxpayer's history of losses with respect to the activity and provides further clarification. Unforeseen or fortuitous circumstances can impact profitability and should be considered.

Treasury Regulation section 1.183-2(b)(7) addresses the occasional profits, if any, that are derived from the activity. The examiner should consider whether there is any reasonable certainty that profits could occur again or if these occasional profits are not likely to be repeated. Insignificant, occasional profits are not indicative of an activity engaged in for profit. However, occasional substantial profit may be indicative of an activity engaged in for profit. The examiner should bear in mind that no one factor is determinative.

In general, a taxpayer that has the potential for falling under the provisions of IRC section 183 will be incurring losses that tend not to diminish with each subsequent year. While depreciation expense may cause losses in the beginning years of the activity's operation, eventually such losses should start to level out as the annual depreciation expense begins to decrease. In other words, the activity's losses will continue to remain the same even though annual depreciation should start to decrease.

The examiner may utilize master file data in order to ascertain a loss history during the pre-examination analysis. Copies of prior year's returns will need to be secured for the case file. Such copies can be obtained from the taxpayer or the taxpayer's representative. Original tax returns may become necessary should a case go forward to the United States Tax Court. At that point, the examiner should defer to Counsel.

LARGE, UNUSUAL, OR QUESTIONABLE ITEMS

Like any other examination, the examiner should consider any large, unusual, or questionable (LUQ) items contained on the Schedule which the activity is reported. In addition to the presence of any LUQ items, the examiner should consider the relationship of certain LUQ items to other items on the Schedule. In the situations where the provisions of IRC section 183 may be applicable, the relationship of any LUQ expense item should be compared to the gross receipts derived from the activity.

For example, minimal gross receipts derived from showing in relation to a significant amount of show-related expenses could be indicative of an activity not engaged in for profit.

GROSS RECEIPTS

Examiners should be alert to the nature of the gross receipts that have been reported on the Schedule. Determine that the income source truly relates to the activity contained on the Schedule. Examiners should also determine that the income source truly exists as some taxpayers have manufactured income in order to make it appear as though the activity earned some income.

Manufactured income raises a potential fraud issue. Examiners should follow local procedures in such instances.

Examiners should also be alert to situations where the reported gross receipts pertain to a bona fide business-type activity, but certain expenses have been deducted which are personal in nature or otherwise nondeductible under IRC section 162. For example, the taxpayer receives gross income from boarding horses for other individuals. The gross receipts are reported correctly on Schedule C or Schedule F. The taxpayer has deducted expenses for show entry fees, transportation to shows, grooming and daycare expenses at the show. These expenses do not pertain to the boarding activity from which the taxpayer derives gross income. During the Initial Interview, the examiner learns that the show related expenses pertain to the taxpayer's personal horses. The show-related expenses are nondeductible under IRC section 162.

The previous example demonstrates how nondeductible expenses can be present among other deductible expenses. While the example does not specifically address the provisions of IRC section 183, the example does lead the examiner to a clue or indication that circumstances do exist that could possibly fall under the provisions of IRC section 183. The examiner needs to follow up and pursue the IRC section 183 potential in greater depth. Personal expenses can be indicative of an activity not engaged in for profit.

OTHER SUBSTANTIAL INCOME SOURCES

Current examination results indicate trends that taxpayers who have the greatest potential for falling under the provisions of IRC section 183 have other substantial income sources outside of the activity in question.

Taxpayers with other substantial income sources generally have the wherewithal to sustain significant financial losses from horse activities or cattle operations. The examiner needs to determine if the taxpayer is sustaining financial losses from the activity in order to offset the other substantial income sources.

The examiner should prepare a spreadsheet that details the tax savings benefit from the operation of the activity. An example of such a spreadsheet is contained in the Appendix of this guide.

Tax Court litigation regarding IRC section 183 has addressed the aspect that certain taxpayers have proven themselves to be capable of financial success in other ventures, but manage to sustain a history of significant financial losses with respect to the activity in question. The tax savings benefit analysis illustrates motivation for the taxpayer to continue an otherwise unprofitable activity.

Factor 1: The Manner in Which the Taxpayer Carries on the Activity

Factor 1 addresses the manner in which the taxpayer carries on the activity. The examiner will document facts and information regarding the taxpayer's activity as derived from the Initial Interview, as well as from the course of the examination process.

Books and Records Used in the Activity

The examiner needs to inquire about the books and records maintained for the activity during the Initial Interview. The examiner should document in the workpapers regarding the sophistication of the taxpayer's books and records. Determine if the taxpayer maintains separate checking accounts for the activity from the taxpayer's personal living expenses.

Depending upon the volume, the examiner should obtain photocopies of the taxpayer's entire set of books and records. If photocopying the entire set of books and records proves to be cost prohibitive, the examiner should only photocopy samples representative of the overall books and records.

Registered breed associations for both cattle and horses offer computer software programs which monitor pedigrees, breeding information, chores, and so forth. In order to register animals with these breed associations, accurate breeding information is mandatory. Cattle breed associations are currently tracking various production data about the registered animals such as birth weights and weaning weights. The examiner needs to determine what type of contemporaneous recordkeeping system the taxpayer uses to record this data. The information provided to the breed association is only as reliable as the contemporaneous field records maintained by the taxpayer. These records must be timely.

The presence of sophisticated books and records does not automatically equate to profit motive. The taxpayer must be relying upon these records in order to operate the activity and make decisions or changes. The examiner needs to document how these records are utilized by the taxpayer. It is not sufficient for the taxpayer to maintain production data, if only for the purpose of satisfying the breed association. The taxpayer should be using the production data in order to determine which animals to keep and breed or which animals to sell. In other words, the taxpayer should not plug production figures in order to satisfy the breed association. This data should be used as a management tool in the daily operation of the activity.

Business Plan

The taxpayer should have a formal written plan. This plan should demonstrate the taxpayer's financial and economic forecast for the activity. The plan should not be a "fantasy Schedule F or C." In other words, some taxpayers may wish to submit a business plan that is nothing more than a Schedule F or C, which unrealistically overstates the gross receipts and unrealistically understates the expenses for the activity. This is not an acceptable business plan.

As previously stated in the text, the examiner should not request the business plan in the first Information Document Request (IDR). Otherwise, the examiner will possibly receive a "canned" document. The examiner should inquire as to the business plan during the Initial Interview and follow-up with a subsequent IDR.

A business plan should show a short range and long range forecast for the activity. The forecast should allow for changes due to potential unforeseen and fortuitous circumstances.

The plan should be realistic. The examiner should perform quantitative analyses in order to determine the reasonableness of the projected gross receipts and various expense items. The examiner may consult with IRS economists in order to review the business plan. The examiner may also consult with local Agricultural Cooperative Extension Agents in order to obtain quantitative formulas to scrutinize the figures projected on the business plan.

For example, the examiner can calculate, with reasonable certainty, the amount of feed required to maintain a certain number of cattle in a particular geographical region. The examiner can start with the taxpayer's projected number of cows required to generate a specific size calf crop. Multiply the number of requisite cows by the amount (in pounds) of feed and hay required to maintain the cows annually. Multiply the pounds of feed by the price per pound for feed.

The examiner can also determine whether the taxpayer's activity would have been profitable if he or she achieved his business plan. For example, a taxpayer has a business plan that includes the goal of maintaining 100 head of cattle in his or her herd. Even if the herd size is increased to 100 head, he or she still could not realize a net profit because he or she could not overcome current operating expenses. Furthermore, the taxpayer does not have sufficient acreage to support

100 of cattle. As such, his or her business plan is not realistic and not likely to generate a net profit.

Methods of Operation

The examiner needs to document the taxpayer's method of operation. As previously mentioned in the text, taxpayers will not operate within the same activity in exactly the same way. The examiner should document the daily operation as well as the history of the activity's operation in the workpapers. Denote changes in the method of operation over the years and indicate why these changes were initiated. Most of this information will be gathered during the Initial Interview.

Efficiency of Operation

The examiner needs to document the efficiency of the taxpayer's operation. Denote the taxpayer's use of any experts or specialists. Indicate if any changes were initiated and why. Obtain names, position titles, and addresses. Most of this information will be gathered during the Initial Interview.

The examiner will denote whether the taxpayer is making changes to the operation that will result in improved operational efficiency. For example, indicate whether production records are used to select animals for removal from the activity. Ask the taxpayer what criteria are used for selecting animals to be used for the activity's program regardless of the activity. Appendix D includes such sample questions.

Issue Identification

The examiner needs to review the actual copy of any advertising in instances where the taxpayer has deducted such expenditures. Many taxpayers will buy advertising space for "vanity" ads. These spaces are frequently purchased to place photographs of their children and the children's horses. The ads wish the children "Best of luck" prior to upcoming show competitions. The examiner should use professional judgment to determine whether the advertisements truly represent promotion of the taxpayer's horse activity.

The examiner needs to be alert for the children's horse activities being deducted on the parents' tax return. The examiner needs to review show reports and determine who actually competes in the horse shows. The parents may contend that the children are promoting the horses for the activity through the show competitions. The examiner needs to consider the substance of the facts. A determination should be made whether the show related expenses are truly recouped through the subsequent sale of any horses. In many instances, great sums of money are expended for show fees, shavings, stall rents, schooling, training, braiding manes and tails, show transportation, travel, and so forth. If and when any horses are sold, the sales price does not justify the means.

Depreciation and Inventory can be viable issues for the examiner to consider as an aside from IRC section 183. The examiner should develop a clear understanding of the taxpayer's activity and verify that the proper tax treatment is used for the horse activity. Horses that are used for breeding purposes are considered depreciable assets. Horses that are held primarily for resale are not depreciable assets.

Example 1

A taxpayer has deducted depreciation expense for show horses because those horses are being "used up" during use in show competitions. However, the taxpayer has also contended that these same show horses are being held for resale. The examiner should consider substance over form and determine whether the horses are being held as inventory for resale or if the horses are depreciable assets.

Examination adjustments for the aforementioned example could impact depreciation expense or the reportable gain on the sale of any horses. This issue can become complex. The examiner should review IRC section 167 for a discussion of depreciation. Most taxpayers who potentially fall under the provisions of IRC section 183 will likely fall outside of the criteria of IRC section 263A due to the amount of the taxpayer's assets.

Summary of Factor 1

The examiner must document the manner in which the taxpayer carries on the activity. Most of this information will be gathered during the Initial Interview and the tour of the operation. It is important for the examiner to document a clear understanding of the activity. Assumptions should not be made that each cattle operation or horse activity operates the same as another similar activity.

Factor 2: The Expertise of the Taxpayer or His or Her Advisors

Factor 2 addresses the expertise of the taxpayer or his or her advisors. The examiner should document the extent to which the taxpayer has relied upon his or her advisors. The examiner should also document the instances where the taxpayer received advice from his or her advisors, but failed to heed this advice.

Decisions and Changes to Operation

The Initial Interview should include questions regarding the taxpayer's expertise, the use of any experts, and any changes or decisions regarding the operation of the activity.

The examiner should establish and document the taxpayer's background in the activity and determine how long the taxpayer has been engaged in the activity. Many times the taxpayer was involved in the activity in some capacity during youth and later became involved again as an adult. These adults have re-entered the activity after they have obtained the financial wherewithal to commence the activity. The examiner should establish a history of the taxpayer's growth of knowledge within the activity and how this knowledge was obtained.

The examiner should establish if the taxpayer has used any advisors or experts in the operation of the activity. Obtain names, position titles, and addresses of these advisors. Document how the advisors were chosen by the taxpayers. Establish the credentials of the advisors. Document if a personal relationship exists between the taxpayer and his advisors.

The examiner needs to document specific instances where the taxpayer was provided advice that was implemented in the activity. Describe how this information affected the operation and any resulting changes. Document whether the advised changes were successful or unsuccessful.

The examiner also needs to document specific instances whereby the taxpayer was advised by his or her experts to make changes and the taxpayer ignored the advice. The examiner should document why the taxpayer chose to ignore this advice. Many taxpayers will provide names of advisors in an effort to demonstrate profit motivation. However, if the taxpayer chooses not to implement the suggested changes and cannot provide just cause for doing so, then the taxpayer's use of advisors is questionable.

Example 2

A taxpayer was advised by his ranch manager to eradicate mesquite brush from a portion of the land. The additional ground would be available for cattle grazing and would allow the taxpayer to increase the size of the herd. A larger herd would result in a larger calf crop and increased potential for additional cattle sales. The taxpayer had the financial wherewithal to eradicate the mesquite brush and the taxpayer's ranch manager was credible. Nonetheless, the taxpayer elected not to follow the advice of the advisor and did not provide any business explanation for his decision. Since the taxpayer also hunted on his ranch, he feared that the eradication would impact the wildlife. In this example, the taxpayer lost credibility with respect to this relevant factor.

Summary of Factor 2

The examiner should document the expertise and knowledge of the taxpayer regarding the activity. The examiner should also document any advisors or experts that the taxpayer has used. Documentation should be prepared which shows specific instances where the taxpayer has followed the advice of the advisor. Documentation should also show how the advice affected the operation of the activity. The examiner should especially note instances when the taxpayer has ignored the recommendations of the advisor and why that decision was made.

Factor 3: The Time and Effort Expended by the Taxpayer in Carrying on the Activity

This factor addresses how much time and effort is expended by the taxpayer in carrying on the activity. In addition to the taxpayer's time, the examiner needs to consider the amount of time expended by any other individuals involved in the activity. The development of this factor may lead to the development of an alternative position under the provisions of IRC section 469 for Passive Activities.

Time and Effort Expended

The examiner needs to establish precisely how much time the taxpayer devotes to this activity as well as all other activities. The amount of time devoted to the activity may be an indicator of profit motive.

If the taxpayer devotes a limited amount of time to the activity, then the taxpayer may be lacking a profit motive. However, if the taxpayer employs competent and qualified individuals to operate the activity, then the taxpayer's time and effort will be reduced.

Time and effort expended reading magazines, journals, and other periodicals is consistent with engaging in a hobby.

Passive Activity Treatment as an Alternative Position

After the examiner determines the amount of time that the taxpayer devotes to the activity, then the examiner should consider the possibility that the provisions under IRC section 469 for Passive Activity may apply to the taxpayer.

If the examiner determines that IRC section 469 may be applicable, then the examiner could use IRC section 469 as an alternative position to IRC section 183.

Issue Identification

The examiner should prepare an analysis that shows how much time is devoted to the activity as well as a breakdown of how that time is spent. For example, the examiner should designate how much is spent attending seminars, reading magazines and journals, or how much time is spent performing repairs and maintenance and so forth.

With respect to an activity that involves show competitions, the "downtime" between the taxpayer's classes in the competition is not counted toward the time calculation. In other words, the time spent waiting between classes or events is not counted.

The examiner should note specifically the amount of time that the taxpayer devotes to other activities.

Summary of Factor 3

The examiner should consider the amount of time that the taxpayer devotes to the activity. The time analysis should precisely detail how much time the taxpayer devotes to each task related to the activity. The examiner should consider whether IRC 469 Passive Activity provisions might be applicable. IRC 469 could provide an alternative position for IRC section 183.

Factor 4: The Expectations That the Assets Used in the Activity May Appreciate in Value

Factor 4 has been the most difficult of the nine relevant factors for examiners to correctly develop. The taxpayer has generally been successful with respect to this factor because of the potential for land appreciation. However, proper development of this factor can overcome the potential for land appreciation.

Single Versus Separate Activities

Factor 4 hinges on whether the operation of the taxpayer's activity and the holding of the land are considered to be a separate or single activity.

According to the Treasury Regulations, Factor 4 states that the term "profit" also includes the appreciation of assets, such as land, used in the activity. An overall profit may occur, in spite of losses from current operations, if the appreciation of the assets is realized.

The examiner needs to prepare an analysis that shows the history of the activity. Beginning with gross receipts, the examiner needs to separate current operating expenses from the costs of carrying the assets. These carrying costs would include depreciation and related interest expense.

The examiner needs to determine if gross receipts exceed current operating expenses with a resulting net profit. For the purpose of this calculation, depreciation expense and related interest expense should be excluded.

As previously mentioned, taxpayers can frequently show potential appreciation of asset value, usually with respect to the land. However, the appreciation of the assets may only be used as a consideration for overall profitably if the operation of the activity and the holding of the assets are considered to be a single activity.

If the operation of the activity and the holding of the assets are considered to be separate activities, then the appreciation of the assets will not be considered for overall profit. In other words, if the operation of the activity and the holding of the assets are considered to be separate activities, the history of operational losses cannot be offset by the potential gain from assets' appreciation.

In order to show that the operation of the activity and the holding of the assets should be treated as separate activities, the examiner needs to refer to the previous analysis. If gross receipts do not exceed current operating expenses, then the operation of the activity and the holding of the assets will be considered as two separate activities. As two separate activities, the history of losses cannot be offset by the appreciation of the assets.

Taxpayer's Intent for Land

Factor 4 relies upon future gain potential to offset current losses. The examiner should inquire during the Initial Interview if the taxpayer intends to retire on the site. Frequently taxpayers have purchased these properties for the purpose of future retirement. If the taxpayer intends to retire on the property, then no future gain will be realized.

Tax Court cases have gone both ways with respect to taxpayers who have expressed retirement purposes as an intention for land acquisition. Nonetheless, the examiner should document such intentions, if known. Since no one factor is determinative by itself, the examiner should address the taxpayer's intention for holding the land.

Computation

First, the examiner needs to begin with gross receipts for each year that the activity has been in operation. Current operating expenses will be deducted from gross receipts in order to determine if there is a current profit or loss from the operation of the activity. Current operating expenses should not include depreciation expense, related interest expense, or real estate taxes for the purpose of this calculation. These expenses would be incurred regardless of the activity.

Issue Identification

The examiner should consider the potential for appreciation of the activity assets, especially the land. This information can be gathered from comparables. Comparables would show land values for properties similar to the taxpayer's parcel. Comparables can be obtained from area realtors. Comparables are extremely important in determining land valuation.

The potential for asset appreciation should be documented on a separate workpaper in the examiner's case file.

Summary of Factor 4

The examiner needs to determine if a potential for asset appreciation exists. The examiner can use comparables for this determination. The examiner also needs to determine whether the operation of the activity and the holding of the land are considered a single activity or separate activities.

In the instances of single activities, the history of losses from current operations will be offset by the future potential gain. In the instances of separate activities, the taxpayer cannot offset current operating losses by future potential gains. A determination of separate activities will result in the taxpayer not meeting Factor 4.

Factor 5: The Success of the Taxpayer in Carrying on Other Similar or Dissimilar Activities

The examiner needs to document the taxpayer's financial success in other activities. This information will be gathered from prior year tax returns as well as the years under examination.

Success in Other Activities

The examiner will prepare a worksheet that details the history of other activities. This detail should show the profits and losses derived from the activities.

In general, many taxpayers have achieved financial success in other business endeavors and yet failed in the operation of the activity in question.

The examiner should focus on activities in addition to the taxpayer's primary source of income. For example, if the taxpayer is a medical doctor, the examiner should not focus on his or her success with his or her medical practice. The examiner should focus on success or failure of other unrelated ventures that were conducted in addition to the medical practice, such as the operation of a restaurant or a kennel.

In addition to the aforementioned worksheet, the examiner needs to document any specific instances where the taxpayer has abandoned certain activities when those activities have proven to be unsuccessful.

Summary of Factor 5

The examiner needs to document the financial successes that the taxpayer has had with other activities. A statement should also address specific instances where the taxpayer has abandoned any activities.

Factor 6: The Taxpayer's History of Income or Losses With Respect to the Activity

The examiner needs to document the history of income or losses generated by the activity. This documentation should be prepared on a detailed worksheet with any narrative as necessary.

While this factor may present the taxpayer in a negative light, examiners should not use this relevant factor by itself in reaching a conclusion regarding the profit motive of the activity.

History of Losses

Some of the nine relevant factors will overlap through the course of the examination process. Information developed for one factor may be used in the development of other factors.

Factor 6 is one of the most important factors of the nine. This factor supports the framework of this Code section.

The examiner needs to prepare a worksheet that shows a history of the activity's profits and losses. The examiner will need to gather prior year tax information using Integrated Data Retrieval System (IDRS). The examiner should order the original returns for any prior years that are no longer "online." These returns would be ordered for review purposes using local procedures.

The examiner can copy the original returns and place them in the administrative file.

The original returns must be secured in the instances where District Counsel proceeds with litigation in United States Tax Court.

Depreciation

The examiner should prepare the worksheet with a separate column that shows the amount of depreciation that was deducted in each tax period. This separation is required for use in the development of other relevant factors.

If the taxpayer has deducted other land carrying costs, such as real estate taxes or related interest expense, then these expenses should be shown in a separate column. Such real estate taxes and mortgage interest would be deductible on Schedule A subject to AGI phase-out limitations.

Summary of Factor 6

IRC section 183 focuses on the lack of profit potential for a specific activity. The question regarding profit motive is initially triggered by history of losses. For this reason, the development of this relevant factor provides the framework for this section. Examiners should not base any conclusions using this relevant factor alone.

Factor 7: The Amount of Occasional Profits, if Any, Which Are Earned

The examiner needs to address the amount of occasional profits that the taxpayer has derived from the activity. In most instances where the provisions of IRC section 183 are considered, the taxpayer will have few profits, if any.

Source of the Income

The examiner needs to consider whether the taxpayer has generated any profits from the activity. A worksheet would be a useful tool in showing these profits or the lack thereof.

The examiner should pinpoint the exact source of the gross receipts reported on the Schedule for the activity on the tax return. There have been instances where taxpayers have misplaced gross receipts, which were derived from sources other than the activity, onto the Schedule for the activity. The misplacement may be an error, or it may be a deliberate attempt to show revenue where revenue did not exist.

If the examiner determines that certain gross receipts were misplaced on the activity's Schedule, the examiner should not include these gross receipts in any of the worksheets prepared for the purpose of developing the IRC section 183 issue. If any worksheets are prepared with the omission of any such gross receipts, a footnote should be included on each worksheet disclosing such omission.

Example 3

A Schedule F for a horse breeding activity contained gross receipts for $3,200. Upon further development, the examiner discovered that the entire amount of the gross receipts pertained to a separate activity, other than the horse breeding. The examiner did not include the $3,200 of misplaced gross receipts in any worksheets during the development of the IRC section 183 issue. The examiner did incorporate footnotes that disclosed that $3,200 of gross receipts was erroneously reported on the Schedule F.

If as in the aforementioned example, a significant sum of gross receipts was misplaced on the activity's Schedule and significant misrepresentation for the profitability results, the examiner should consider the implications of such misplacement. Civil fraud may be a consideration depending upon the overall impact.

If the examiner in the previous example had not excluded the misplaced gross receipts from the various IRC section 183 worksheets, then a true picture of the taxpayer's activity would not have been portrayed.

Some taxpayers have fabricated income for the activity in an effort to put forth an appearance of profit motive. The examiner needs to verify the income. Such fabrication raises consideration of potential fraud. Examiners should follow local procedures in such instances.

Summary of Factor 7

The examiner should consider the amount of occasional profits that the activity may generate. However, the examiner should determine the source of the gross receipts just in case the gross receipts have been misplaced on the tax return. Such misplacement could misstate the profitability of the activity and should be removed from the IRC section 183 issue development with footnotes or disclosures to that effect.

Factor 8: The Financial Status of the Taxpayer

This factor addresses the financial status of the taxpayer. In some instances, the taxpayer may have the financial wherewithal to sustain a history of financial losses for the activity. Certain taxpayers may receive a tax benefit from the losses incurred by the activity as these losses will offset other substantial sources of income.

Other Substantial Sources of Income

In general, taxpayers with other substantial sources of income have the financial wherewithal to sustain significant losses from activities that appear to meet the criteria of the provisions set forth under IRC section 183.

Taxpayer propaganda has been written that advises taxpayers to enter into horse activities for the purpose of deriving a tax benefit. Some of the propaganda has referred to such participation as "horse shelters." There are no sections of the Internal Revenue Code that address tax shelters for horse activities. The propagandists have based their theory upon the language of IRC section 183 with respect to horse activities and played within the gray areas to suit their purpose.

In general, horse activities are not inexpensive. Taxpayers with other substantial sources of income have the financial wherewithal to enter such activities irrespective of the motivation. The examiner needs to understand why the taxpayer has not abandoned an unsuccessful activity when other taxpayers who lack the same financial wherewithal would most likely abandon the unprofitable activity.

Many Tax Court cases have been pursued which involve taxpayers that have other substantial sources of income that have engaged in historically unprofitable horse or cattle operations without abandonment. In general, taxpayers who have other substantial sources of income have not faired as well in Tax Court litigation as taxpayers who do not have such financial wherewithal.

Issue Identification

The examiner needs to document the financial status of the taxpayer in the workpapers. The examiner should also make a statement to the effect that the financial status has enabled the taxpayer to sustain a history of losses in the activity.

Earlier text directed the examiner to prepare a tax savings benefit analysis. This spreadsheet would show possible motivation for certain taxpayers to continue participation in an unsuccessful financial endeavor.

Summary of Factor 8

In general, taxpayers who have other substantial sources of income have the financial wherewithal to sustain a history of losses with respect to cattle or horse activities. Some taxpayers actually derive a tax benefit from participation in these activities since the losses offset the other sources of substantial income.

Factor 9: The Elements of Personal Pleasure or Recreation

Section 183 has been referred to as the "hobby loss" section because many taxpayers have engaged in unprofitable activities due to the pleasurable attributes of the activities. Factor 9 addresses the elements of personal pleasure or recreation of the activity.

Pleasurable or Recreational Aspects

The examiner must develop an understanding of the taxpayer's activity. This understanding must be documented in the workpapers. The examiner must document all tasks that the taxpayer performs within the activity.

Some taxpayers will attempt to downplay any pleasurable aspects of the activity. Some will attempt to portray the activity as laborious with emphasis placed on the drudgery. These taxpayers know where the examination is leading. They will emphasize the labor to clean or muck the stalls. The examiner needs to understand that if these taxpayers care about their animals that any such task is a labor of love or concern for the well being of the animal.

Many individuals who have not participated in horse or cattle operations readily buy into the "drudgery concept" set forth by certain taxpayers. Individuals who have participated in such activities put aside the drudgery concept because they see the overall picture. These animals are loved so they receive loving care regardless of the effort required.

The examiner should realize that cattle and horse activities provide numerous opportunities for social outlets. Breed association field days and auctions provide social interaction with other breeders. Breeders also find peace and solace from watching their herd grazing in the pasture. The animals can be a source of beauty to behold in an environment of peace and tranquility. Great pride and satisfaction can be derived from the accomplishments achieved. Breeders enjoy watching the new baby offspring romping and playing in the pastures.

Many taxpayers will express a passion for their activity. A skilled examiner will be able to draw this passion from the taxpayer through conversation.

The Internal Revenue Code does not mandate that taxpayers cannot enjoy the method by which they derive their income. Many taxpayers resist the phraseology of "hobby loss" in reference to IRC section 183. As previously mentioned, examiners may wish to refrain from that terminology and refer to the actual title "Activity Not Engaged in for Profit."

Issue Identification

The examiner needs to listen carefully to the taxpayer's discussion of the activity. Both cattle and horse activities provide opportunities for social interaction with other breeders or participants. The thrill of competition draws participants into various shows and competitive events. A sense of accomplishment attracts participants to compete in events where there may not be any monetary compensation for their efforts. Great pride accompanies the receipt of large trophies and fancy rosette ribbons and award banners.

Summary of Factor 9

The examiner needs to address the pleasurable and recreational aspects of the activity. The examiner should remember that taxpayers are willing to overlook the drudgery of certain tasks when the pleasurable aspects outweigh the negatives. An individual who loves his or her animals will willingly provide loving care.

By this point in the examination, the taxpayer is aware of the direction that the exam is going. The taxpayer knows about the nine relevant factors. A taxpayer with a savvy representative has been advised to downplay the pleasurable aspects and emphasize the drudgery and dirty work of the activity. Skilled listening will help the examiner to document and sort the details regarding this relevant factor.

COMPLIANCE ISSUES

Unique compliance issues will be discussed. Where applicable, information will be included on these areas of noncompliance:

- Underreporting of income
- Employment taxes
- IRP document compliance
- Misplaced income sources

Underreporting of Income

Incomplete books and records may lead to the underreporting of income. Sales Invoices from the sale barn may not be retained in a manner to facilitate correct income computations. Checks from the sale barn for the sale of cull animals may be de minimis in dollar value. These inconsequential checks are frequently not deposited into bank accounts, but are cashed. Small cull sales may be significant in the aggregate. The examiner may need to engage an indirect method to reveal unreported sales.

The examiner should be aware that sale barns are not currently required to issue Forms 1099 for horse and cattle sales.

One indirect method could be based on the herd inventory where every available producing animal and resulting offspring are counted. Another indirect method could be developed from the Feed Expense. The examiner could project the number of animals fed based upon checking the feed consumption. The local Agricultural Extension Agent can provide formulas that consider the annual feed consumption of an animal. This formula will enable the examiner to project feed costs over the entire herd. The examiner should consider the facts and circumstances of the taxpayer in determining whether all gross income has been correctly reported and developing alternative methods in the instances where gross income may be understated.

Employment Taxes

Many of the taxpayers who potentially fall under the provisions of IRC section 183 are involved in business ventures other than the horse activity or cattle operation. In fact, these taxpayers may derive a substantial amount of income from these ventures and devote a great deal of time to the primary sources of their income. As a result, third parties are engaged to perform the labor for the horse and cattle activities. Depending on the locale of the horse or cattle activity, undocumented laborers may be used. Other employment tax issues may result from failure to file Forms 1099. Employee classification issues may also be present.

IRP Document Compliance

The taxpayer may fail to report all sources of income per reconciliation of the IRP document. Such failure may be deliberate or the result of incomplete records. The taxpayer may also miscategorize income derived from another source on the Schedule for the horse or cattle activity in an effort to show income for that activity.

Misplaced Income Sources

As mentioned in the previous paragraph, taxpayers may misplace income sources in an effort to show income for the horse or cattle activity. This may or may not result in a net profit for the activity.

The examiner needs to examine the compilation of reported gross receipts for the activity. Misplaced income items may need to be moved to the correct schedule in order to achieve the appropriate tax treatment for the transaction.

The examiner also needs to consider the implications of any misplaced income items, especially when the impact is significant.

Example 4

Income derived from working at a florist shop was placed on the Schedule for a horse activity. The horse activity had no other sources of income. As a result, the horse activity appeared to be generating income.

This discussion of issues is not all-inclusive. Examiners should be aware of new and emerging issues within the horse and cattle industries. Local MSSP Specialists can assist examiners with changing trends.

This page was left intentionally blank.

Chapter 3

Examination Techniques

PURPOSE

This chapter covers the techniques specific to examining the issues identified in the previous chapter.

The development of the IRC section 183 issue is a fact-gathering process. The Treasury Regulations provide further guidance through nine relevant factors. In order to adequately develop IRC section 183, the examiner needs to address the nine relevant factors during the Initial Interview. The Regulations indicate that no single factor determines whether the activity is engaged in for profit. The examiner needs to consider all of the factors and draw a conclusion based upon the examiner's professional judgment.

In addition to the nine relevant factors, the examiner also needs to develop a full understanding of the taxpayer's activity and the extent of the taxpayer's involvement in the activity. It is not enough for the examiner to know that a taxpayer is involved in a horse activity or cattle operation. The examiner needs to understand what specific type of horse activity or cattle operation the taxpayer is engaged.

INFORMATION DOCUMENT REQUEST (IDR)

Shown below are some documents examiners may want to consider when preparing an Information Document Request (IDR). Not all of these items should be requested in every case. Not all items would be requested on the first IDR. Some items may be appropriately requested on a subsequent IDR. Examiners should use this information as a guide and request only the items that are appropriate and relevant for their specific case:

• Registration certificates for animals, if applicable
• A copy of the herd inventory for the year of examination
• Supporting documentation for all expenses deducted on Schedule C/F
• Business plan for activity

Issue Identification

Reviewing the tax return will provide the first issues for further development by the examiner. These issues would include any large, unusual, or questionable (LUQ) items contained on the Schedule pertaining to the activity. These LUQ items would be addressed during the Initial Interview and the Information Document Request.

When considering LUQ items, the examiner needs to inspect the relationship of any showing expenses to the overall Schedule C or F. A significant amount of showing and showing-related expenses could be indicative of an activity not engaged in for profit if the prizes are minimal in financial remuneration. The examiner needs to determine the specific purpose for which the taxpayer participates in show competitions. The examiner needs to determine if the show winnings justify the showing expenses. If the taxpayer's activity is a showing activity, then all of the expenses would be related to showing. If the taxpayer's showing activity is not generating sufficient prize money, then the profit motive should be considered.

The examiner should consider the gross receipts for the activity. The tax return may have minimal or zero gross receipts. The activity's history of gross receipts should be addressed. The examiner needs to determine why there have been minimal or no gross receipts. The examiner needs to determine specifically when the taxpayer expects for gross receipts to increase and specifically how the taxpayer expects to accomplish this.

Examiners need to verify all expenses that pertain to the activity's Schedule C or F. The examiner needs to prepare a worksheet which details any personal expenses contained within these Schedules. The worksheet should detail whether the expenses were fully substantiated. This worksheet would be necessary if the case should close "unagreed" at the Group level. The information would be useful in preparing alternative positions.

Using Specialists and Other Resources

Specialists and other outside resources can provide assistance in developing IRC section 183 issues. These specialists can come from within the Internal Revenue Service or from outside of the organization.

IRS specialists could include farming industry specialists, Market Segment Specialty Program agents or Economists. Industry specialist and MSSP agents would be able to provide insight regarding industry specifics. Economists would be able to provide guidance regarding the economic feasibility of the taxpayer's business plans. District economists may be formally assigned to a specific case or the examiner may informally contact them.

The current Internal Revenue Code dictates that the taxpayer must be notified prior to the examiner's contact of third parties. This notification is required if the examiner should ask specific questions about specific taxpayers. If the examiner should choose to ask a generic question which does not pertain to a specific taxpayer by name, then this notification process is not required. For example, the examiner could inquire of an Agricultural Cooperative Extension Agent as to the recommended number of cattle per acre for a certain county. This inquiry does not identify a specific taxpayer by name. Furthermore, the examiner could gather breed information from a breed association's Web site on the Internet (in District's where such access is available). These requests do not fall under the notification guidelines.

In the Districts where Internet access is available, the Internet can also serve as another resource for information. The examiner can obtain general information about the taxpayer's breed of cattle or horse from the breed association's Web page. Some taxpayers may have a Web Site for their activity.

INITIAL INTERVIEW

A sample questionnaire has been provided in the Appendix. This questionnaire is comprised of questions to consider asking at the Initial Interview. Not all of these questions are warranted in every case. Examiners should use them as a guide and ask only those questions that are appropriate for the specific examination. Some questions pertain only to horse activities while others pertain only to cattle operations.

The examiner should note that the sample Initial Interview contains questions that are pertinent for certain methods of conducting these activities. For example, some questions are specifically directed to commercial cattle operations while other questions are specifically directed to herds registered with a recognized breed association.

The examiner should request the taxpayer's presence for the Initial Interview because the Power of Attorney generally will not have intimate knowledge of the taxpayer's method of operation. While some Powers of Attorney will try to handle the Initial Interview without the taxpayer's presence, the taxpayer is the best resource regarding the activity. The Initial Interview should contain very specific questions regarding the activity.

If a Power of Attorney attempts to conduct the Initial Interview without the taxpayer present, do not accept responses from the POA which appear to be "guesses." Some answers may appear to be "canned" or broadly unspecific to the examiner's taxpayer. These "guesses" and "canned responses" will not serve the taxpayer fairly. At such a point, the examiner should ask the Power of Attorney to reconsider the taxpayer's participation for the meeting.

During the Initial Interview, the examiner should discuss the taxpayer's Business Plan for the activity. Do not request the Business Plan on the Information Document Request with the first appointment letter or the examiner will receive a "canned document." The examiner wants to develop candid and spontaneous responses from the taxpayer during the Initial Interview. The formal Business Plan should be requested on a subsequent Information Document Request. If the taxpayer indicates that no formal written Business Plan exists, or has ever existed, the examiner must document this fact in the interview workpapers.

Refer to the Issues chapter for a full discussion of the formal Business Plan.

Sample Initial Interview questions will be listed in the Appendix. These questions can provide a reference; however, the examiner will want to customize the questions to suit the specific taxpayer.

The Initial Interview should gather detailed information about the taxpayer's activity. The examiner should not generalize all taxpayers that participate in horse activities or cattle operations. Each taxpayer conducts his or her respective activity differently from others in the same activity. The Initial Interview should document and detail specific information.

EXAM LOCATION AND BUSINESS TOUR

There are special aspects of the market segment that need to be observed during the tour of the business facility. These observations will be made in correlation with the nine relevant factors set forth in the Treasury Regulations for IRC section 183.

Tour of Operation

Tours of the taxpayer's operation can be a very helpful tool in the examination process. Tours can help the examiner develop an understanding as to the operation of the activity since methodology could vary. Assumptions about activities should never be made because each taxpayer could operate differently.

The examiner should be aware that a tour of the operation could possibly impair the examiner's perception of the taxpayer's level of expertise. For example, if the taxpayer's expertise regarding the activity exceeds the examiner's expertise in the same activity, the examiner could incorrectly conclude that the taxpayer has met Factor 2 of the nine relevant factors in the Regulations. That aspect will be discussed further later in the text.

Prior to the tour of the operation, the examiner should decide whether the assistance of an IRS Farm Specialist would be beneficial. This decision would be based upon the examiner's comfort level with the taxpayer's activity. An IRS Farming Specialist could attend the tour of operation with the examiner. Upon the conclusion of the tour, the specialist could provide the examiner with recommendations for further development of the IRC section 183 issue. The specialist would also provide another professional opinion as to the presence of the issue.

The examiner should make note of the overall first impression of the activity's facility. The examiner should observe the condition of the structures and fences. Are they in good condition or disrepair? Will the condition of the structures and fences serve the purpose intended? Would any animals be able to escape from the fenced-in area? Could the animals become harmed due to the inadequacy of the structures or fences?

The examiner should not let the presence of fancy buildings, barns, and expensive fence influence an opinion regarding the profit motive of the activity. Expensive barns, fences, and equipment do not automatically equate to a business engaged in for profit. Such items, when purchased for a hobby activity, are indicative of the taxpayer's affluent taste and preferences, not profit motivation.

In addition to the first impression of the activity's facilities, the examiner should exercise professional judgment and ascertain the taxpayer's familiarity of the facilities. This determination can be made if the taxpayer is present for the tour. The taxpayer's familiarity could be an indicator of the level of participation within the activity. The taxpayer's knowledge and expertise, or lack thereof, could become evident during the tour.

The examiner needs to be careful not to be influenced by the taxpayer's knowledge or expertise merely because that knowledge or expertise exceeds that of the examiner's. While many taxpayers may have basic knowledge requisite of that particular activity, the basic knowledge does not equate to a profit motivation nor does it demonstrate that the taxpayer has the knowledge or ability to operate the activity like a business with a profit motive. Many hobbyists possess a wealth of knowledge regarding their activities.

Furthermore, the taxpayer may indeed possess basic knowledge of the activity and yet proceed to exercise some very poor decisions with respect to that activity. Some decisions might be so poor that other taxpayers within the same activity would consider those decisions extremely inappropriate and incorrect.

Example 1

taxpayer states that he sold his entire herd of registered cattle so that he could start over with a commercial cattle herd. Upon the complete dispersal of the registered animals, the taxpayer purchased commercial grade cattle. The cattle were fully depreciated. That decision was inappropriate and incorrect. If the taxpayer had stopped registering the offspring with the breed association, then the taxpayer would have turned his herd into a commercial cattle herd. The taxpayer did not need to disperse an entire herd in order to accomplish the goal of attaining a commercial herd.

The aforementioned example serves to show that taxpayers may exercise inappropriate decisions in spite of the basic knowledge possessed. Examiners should not be intimidated if the taxpayer's knowledge exceeds their own. Furthermore, examiners should not prematurely conclude that the taxpayer is engaging in the activity for the sake of a profit just because the taxpayer possesses knowledge of the activity.

The examiner should be aware that taxpayers could make preparations for the tour of operation that would result in a misrepresentation of the activity.

Example 2

A taxpayer that does not really maintain a certain number of cattle could have cattle trucked to the location for the purpose of the examiner's tour. Such cattle in this scenario would probably not belong to the taxpayer or the taxpayer may have recently purchased these animals at the sale barn for the purpose of the operation tour.

Example 3

An Appeals Officer viewed videotape of the taxpayer's beef cattle operation. The Appeals Officer observed that the cattle in the video were Holstein dairy cows and not the taxpayer's designated beef breed. The taxpayer decided to concede the IRC section 183 issue after that point.

The examiner should be alert that cattle could be shipped in for the examiner's tour. An examiner should look at the cattle to determine if the eartags follow the taxpayer's herd inventory. The examiner should cross match the herd inventory and attempt to locate a sample from within the herd. If the examiner cannot locate any animals from the sample, then the sample should be expanded. The examiner should inquire where these animals are located. The examiner should exercise professional judgment if it becomes apparent that the herd inventory does not tie to the physical inventory in the pasture. Death could account for some missing cattle. The examiner should consider the impact if the cattle have been misrepresented.

When the examiner views the livestock, the examiner should observe whether the animals are readily identifiable and distinguishable from one another through the use of eartags or other similar markings. The presence of a brand on the animals serves to identify ownership of the livestock. If the animals were acquired from another breeder, then the brand of the original owner might still be on the animals. The eartags would serve to identify the individual animal from all other animals in the herd and permit the taxpayer to maintain performance records on each individual animal. The numbers on the eartags should be separate and distinct. In other words, the herd should not contain two animals with the same ear number. The examiner may wish to sample eartag numbers to test the taxpayer's recordkeeping. The examiner could ask to review the performance records of those animals sampled. The significance of performance records will be discussed in greater detail later in the text.

In addition to the observation of eartags, the examiner should also observe how many breeding males are present within the herd. Purebred associations mandate that the breeding females should only be exposed to one breeding male at any one time. This regulation ensures that the true parentage of any offspring is known to be correct and guarantees the accuracy of that offspring's pedigree for registration purposes.

With respect to commercial herds (where the offspring are not registered through a recognized breed association), the taxpayer should still refrain from exposing the breeding females to more than one breeding male at any one time. The taxpayer needs to know with certainty which breeding male has sired each offspring in order to evaluate the performance of each breeding male. Breeding males need to be removed from the breeding program if that particular breeding male is not producing desirable offspring.

The taxpayer may argue that he or she can determine which breeding male sired which offspring based upon the color of the offspring. This defense is not genetically valid. For example, the taxpayer may have one black stud and one red stud. The females may be of any color. If the taxpayer releases both studs into the herd at the same time, the color of the resulting offspring cannot be used to determine paternity because of the color genetics present in the females' ancestry. The red stud may still produce a black offspring if there was any black in the female's ancestry. If perhaps the red stud had black in his ancestry, then resulting offspring could be of either color.

During the course of the tour, the examiner should make notes of the observations as well as questions for further follow-up. Some examiners may wish to take photographs with the permission of the taxpayer.

The examiner should observe the condition under which the taxpayer stores the hay for the livestock. If the taxpayer does not adhere to local suggested methods, the examiner should consider the taxpayer's knowledge or expertise. Perhaps the taxpayer's use of unsuitable methods is an indication of the taxpayer's lack of concern for the activity's profitability. The examiner should consult with local agricultural specialists for recommended methods. In general, hay should be stored in such a way that it does not get wet and mold. While large, round bales may be maintained in the fields, they should be covered with some type of fabric covering to protect from moisture. Spoiled hay could present health problems for the animals. Cattle are less at risk, but horses can develop colic and die from poor quality hay. Poor quality hay is low in nutritive value, which would result in poor growth of the animal consuming such hay. Poor growth results in more cost for the taxpayer in order to achieve market weights for cattle. Increased costs reduce the overall profit for the activity.

The examiner should observe the physical condition of the taxpayer's animals. The examiner should consider whether the animals appear to be well fed or underfed. The technical process of assessing an animal's flesh condition is sometimes referred to as body scoring. Local cooperative agricultural extension agents can provide guidance as to how body scoring is determined for both horses and cattle. The examiner will probably not need to compute condition scores during the examination process. Nonetheless, the examiner needs to comment as to the overall flesh condition. Flesh condition and condition scores have been proven indicators of an animal's reproductive abilities. Impaired reproductive abilities reduce the activity's profitability if breeding is a component of the activity. In other words, animals that receive poor nutrition are less capable of successful reproduction and impaired reproduction affects the activity's bottom line.

The animal's body condition should be considered as an indication of the taxpayer's involvement in the activity. An absentee owner may not be aware of the care that an animal is receiving. There have been several incidents whereby absentee owners have neglected their livestock and the animals have been known to starve to death. Some livestock have contracted an illness or disease of which the absentee owner was not aware. Lack of timely medical intervention has resulted in death. These occurrences do not mean that every absentee owner neglects his or her livestock. In fact, the absentee owner may have hired a competent manager. The hired manager may or may not be competent or reliable. The absentee owner should stay on top of the activity and intervene when the hired manager fails to adequately perform his or her duties. Absentee ownership, as it lends to an alternative position for passive activity, will be discussed in greater detail later in the text.

Alternatives to Operation Tours for Tax Auditors

Tax Auditors do not have the opportunity to perform a physical tour of the taxpayer's activity. However, the Tax Auditor can inspect any photographs that the taxpayer may have of the facility or of any animals owned by the taxpayer. The Tax Auditor will have to use professional judgment in gauging the authenticity of the photographs. Remember that the photographs are going to reflect the best side of the activity. Any unflattering photographs will not be shown to the Tax Auditor.

Tax Auditors will find Agricultural Cooperative Extension Agents very helpful resources. These County Agents can tell the Tax Auditors how many animals per acre should be carried in a particular area of a specific county. The Tax Auditor can then determine if the taxpayer has sufficient land in order to carry the requisite animals needed to generate adequate revenue.

Tax Auditors can also consult with any district Revenue Agent who may specialize in the farming issues. If circumstances warrant, perhaps a District MSSP Specialist could perform the operation tour and report back to the Tax Auditor.

The Tax Auditor will rely upon interviewing skills in order to develop the facts. Since IRC section 183 cases are fact gathering intensive, Tax Auditors are not completely hindered even though they cannot perform field tours.

UNIQUE INDIRECT METHODS

The development of IRC section 183 Farm Hobby Loss cases could use Indirect Methods for certain aspects of case development. A discussion of unique indirect methods follows. This includes creative methodologies developed for the market segment such as:

• Gross-up on feed purchases
• Potential sales based upon breeding herd inventory

The use of financial status audit techniques should be limited to situations where the IRS already has indications of unreported income.

BOOKS AND RECORDS

Horse activities and cattle operations have unique methods of recordkeeping which serve to track the performance of each animal. These records should be used as management tools to enable the taxpayer to make informed business decisions.

SOURCES OF INFORMATION

There are numerous sources of information about horse activities and cattle operations. These include:

• Breed associations
• Memberships in cattle and horse associations other than breed associations
• Local County Agricultural Extension Agents
• Other ATGs and reference material (Internal Revenue Service publications, periodicals, etc.).

3-9

OTHER

The examiner may need to use a summons in order to obtain corroborating information from third parties. The examiner will need to refer to current local procedures for third party notification.

Chapter 4

Supporting Law

PURPOSE

This chapter provides the examiner with the legal support for the issues including:
- Internal Revenue Code
- Treasury Regulations
- Court Cases
- Coordinated Issue Papers

INTERNAL REVENUE CODE

Internal Revenue Code section 183 provides guidance.

The general rule under IRC section 183 states that "in the case of an activity engaged in by an individual or an S Corporation, if such activity is not engaged in for profit, no deduction attributable to such activity shall be allowed under this chapter except as provided in this section".

This section does not apply to C Corporations.

IRC section 183(c) defines an activity not engaged in for profit as any activity other than one with respect to which deductions are allowable for the taxable year under IRC section 162 or under paragraph (1) or (2) of IRC section 212. In other words, this section refers to an activity to which deductions are not deductible under IRC section 162 or under paragraph (1) or (2) of IRC section 212.

IRC section 183(d) defines the presumption that addresses the number of years for which an entity should observe a profit during a period of consecutive taxable years. For the purpose of this text, cattle operations must observe a profit for 3 or more taxable years during a period of 5 consecutive taxable years. Horse activities such as breeding, training, showing, or racing must observe a profit in 2 of 7 consecutive taxable years.

TREASURY REGULATIONS

Treasury Regulation section 1.183-(2)(b)(1) through (9) provides guidance through nine relevant factors for consideration of the applicability of IRC section 183. All nine factors must be considered when determining if an activity is engaged in for profit. No one factor is determinative; however, the more factors in the Government's favor, the better. The nine relevant factors will be discussed in the following summary. Refer to the Issues chapter for greater development of the factors.

Activity Not Engaged In For Profit

Treasury Regulation section 1.183-2(b)(1) through (9)

1) Manner in which the taxpayer carries on the activity.

The fact that the taxpayer carries on the activity in a businesslike manner may indicate that the activity may be engaged in for profit. Determine whether the taxpayer maintains complete and accurate books and records. Changes in operating methods, adoption of new techniques, and abandonment of unprofitable methods may also indicate a profit motive.

It should be noted whether the taxpayer actually uses these books and records as a management tool whereby decisions regarding the activity are made from these records.

2) The expertise of the taxpayer or his advisors.

Preparation for the activity through extensive study of accepted business, economic, and scientific practices, or consultation with experts may indicate that the taxpayer has a profit motive where the taxpayer adheres to such practices.

The examiner should also denote specific instances where the taxpayer has not followed the recommendations of his advisors and why.

3) The time and effort expended by the taxpayer in carrying on the activity.

The fact that the taxpayer devotes much of his personal time and effort to carrying on the activity, particularly if the activity does not have much substantial personal or recreational aspects, may indicate an intention to derive a profit.

4) Expectation that assets used in the activity may appreciate in value.

The term "profit" encompasses appreciation in the value of assets used in the activity. Thus, the taxpayer may intend to derive a profit from the operation of the activity when appreciation in the value of the assets used in the activity exceeds operation expenses.

Taxpayer's goal: Show that the activity and the holding of the asset = single activity.

Examiner's goal: Show that the activity and the holding of the asset = separate activities.

Why?

Single activity – The taxpayer may offset the potential gain from the sale of assets against the history of losses. Examiners should utilize land comparables to verify potential appreciation.

Separate activities – The taxpayer cannot offset the history of losses against the potential appreciation.

How?

The examiner begins with the Schedule F (C) and removes any expenses associated with the carrying costs of the land, such as taxes and mortgage interest. Only current operating costs should be remaining. Determine whether Gross Receipts exceeds the current operating costs. If current operations generate a net profit, then the holding of the land and the operation of the activity are considered to be a single activity. If Gross Receipts do not exceed current operating costs and a net loss is derived, then the holding of the land and the activity are considered to be separate activities.

5) The success of the taxpayer in other similar/dissimilar activities.

The fact that the taxpayer has engaged in similar activities in the past and converted these activities from unprofitable to profitable enterprises may indicate that the taxpayer has engaged in the present activity for profit, regardless of current profitability.

However, the examiner should address why the taxpayer, who has been of financial success with other endeavors, can suffer a history of losses and lack of financial success with the activity under consideration. Furthermore, the examiner should consider why the taxpayer has not abandoned the activity in spite of historical losses.

For example, a business executive has derived financial success from several business ventures. However, his horse activity has continuously generated significant net losses. The examiner should address why an executive, who possesses the business savvy to generate substantial profits from other ventures, has been unable to generate a profit from the activity under consideration.

6) The taxpayer's history of income or losses with respect to the activity.

A series of losses during the initial start-up of any activity may not necessarily be an indication that the activity is not engaged in for profit. However, when losses continue to be sustained beyond the normal start-up period, such losses may be an indication that the activity is not engaged in for profit.

If the losses were sustained due to unforeseen or fortuitous circumstances, such losses would not be indication that the activity is not engaged in for profit. Fortuitous circumstances may include depressed market conditions. The examiner should consider whether the taxpayer has made any concessions to change his business plan and marketing strategy in times of a depressed market.

7) The amount of occasional profits, if any, which are earned.

The opportunity to earn a substantial profit in a highly speculative venture may be sufficient to indicate that the activity is engaged in for profit. The examiner should ascertain whether the taxpayer performed any significant investigative work prior to the commencement of the activity. Refer to Factor One.

8) The financial status of the taxpayer.

Substantial income from other sources may indicate that the activity is not engaged in for profit, especially if there are personal or recreational elements involved. The taxpayer may also derive a tax benefit from any losses generated from the activity. Some taxpayers with affluent lifestyles enjoy participating in certain activities, such as horse breading, and have the financial wherewithal to do so.

9) Elements of personal pleasure or recreation.

The presence of personal motives in carrying on an activity may indicate that the activity is not engaged in for profit. This may be especially true when there are recreational or personal elements involved. The Internal Revenue

Code does not preclude the taxpayer from enjoying the activity in which he is engaged. However, the taxpayer should not allow personal pleasure or recreation to prevent abandonment of an otherwise unprofitable activity.

CASE LAW

There are innumerable United States Tax Court cases for IRC section 183 Farm Hobby Losses. Some cases have been favorable for the taxpayer while other cases have supported the Government. The volume would extend beyond the breadth of this text.

The examiner should cite cases on point that have specific facts that match the facts of the taxpayer currently under examination. The examiner should also note unfavorable cases to the Government on which the taxpayer may rely. The examiner should request that the Power of Attorney provide a list of the cites of court cases which defend the taxpayer's position.

COORDINATED ISSUE PAPER

At the time of this writing, there are not any Coordinated Issue Papers for this market segment.

This page left intentionally blank.

Appendix

This appendix provides additional information that will assist the examiner with the development of IRC section 183 Farm Hobby Loss cases. These sample SHEETS INCLUDE

Appendix A • Calculating the examination adjustments per IRC section 183

Appendix B • Alternative positions

Appendix C • General Suspense and IRC section 183(e) procedures

Appendix D • Sample Initial Interview

Appendix E • Tax Savings Benefit Analysis

This page left intentionally blank.

CALCULATING THE EXAMINATION ADJUSTMENT
PER IRC section 183

When the examiner has determined that the taxpayer falls under the provisions of IRC section 183, the section provides guidance in calculating the examination adjustment using an ordering principle.

The actual adjustments have been frequently computed incorrectly. This portion of the text will lead the examiner through the correct calculation.

INCORRECT COMPUTATION OF ADJUSTMENT

A common error in computing the IRC section 183 adjustment involves a simplistic approach, which makes logical sense, but is incorrect nonetheless.

Examiners have started with Gross Receipts and deducted expenses to the extent of Gross Receipts using the ordering principle; however, examiners have frequently failed to move Mortgage Interest, Real Estate taxes, and casualty expenses over to Schedule A subject to AGI limitations.

The following example shows the **incorrect** method of computation. **Examiners should not use this method of computation!**

Gross Receipts	5,400.00
- Expenses (Mortgage Interest)	4,800.00
- Expenses (Supplies, Repairs, Etc.)	600.00
= Balance of Gross Receipts	0.00
Remaining Expenses = Adjustment	24,000.00

ORDERING PRINCIPLE

Treasury Regulation section 1.183-1(b)(i) through (iii) provides guidance using the ordering principle with respect to allowable deductions.

Begin with the activity's Gross Receipts for the current taxable year. Allowable deductions will not exceed the Gross Receipts for the activity.

The Treasury Regulations allow expenses to be deducted in the following order:

1. Mortgage interest, taxes, and casualty losses.
2. Expenses that do not reduce basis such as Supplies, Utilities, and other such expenses.

3. Depreciation and amortization expenses.

It should be noted that other sections of the Internal Revenue Code might also be applicable during the ordering process and further limit the deductibility of certain expenses. For example, Interest Expense may be further limited under IRC section 163(d).

The examiner needs to evaluate the expenses deducted on the Schedule C or F and place these expenses in the aforementioned order. A separate worksheet is helpful in preparing the adjustment.

MORTGAGE INTEREST AND REAL ESTATE TAXES

Mortgage interest, real estate taxes, and casualty losses top the list because these items would be deductible elsewhere on the tax return. Since these items are deductible elsewhere, the examiner's first step is to move these expenses over to Schedule A, deductible subject to the limitations of AGI phaseout.

DEDUCTIONS TO THE EXTENT OF GROSS RECEIPTS

The amount of expenses moved to Schedule A are deducted from Gross Receipts that may or may not fully absorb Gross Receipts. If any portion of Gross Receipts remains for absorption, then the examiner will allow a deduction for expenses which do not reduce basis, such as Supplies, Utilities, and so forth. These expenses are generally current expenses for the activity.

If any Gross Receipts are left for absorption after the deduction of the aforementioned expenses, then the examiner will allow the deduction for Depreciation and amortization expenses.

In most instances, Gross Receipts are not adequate for the deduction of all expenses as deducted per return. To the extent that the expenses exceed Gross Receipts, an adjustment is made to disallow the extra expenses.

ALTERNATIVE POSITIONS

It is always prudent for an examiner to be prepared to present an Alternative Position with any unagreed report. IRC section 183 positions are no exception. There are several viable alternative positions that are companions to the IRC section 183 position. IRC section 162 Business Expenses should be addressed in all IRC section 183 cases. Section 469 for Passive Activity Losses may be applicable to the taxpayer at hand.

Many times the IRC section 162 alternative issue is not fully developed. The examiner should first substantiate the income and expenses. Then the examiner should make a determination regarding ordinary and necessary with respect to the expense items.

Depreciation Expense may require some significant overhaul depending upon the taxpayer's intent for the animals used in the activity. Many errors have been incurred within the proper tax treatment of the animals. Previous text addressed problems with this issue.

LEGAL PRESUMPTION

An activity shall be presumed to be engaged in for profit if the gross income derived from the activity for three (or two if applicable*) or more of the taxable years in such period exceeds the deductions attributable to the activity.

* Note: In the case of an activity that consists of breeding, training, showing, or racing of horses, the activity shall be presumed to be engaged in for profit if the gross income derived from the activity for two or more of the taxable years in such period exceeds the deductions attributable to the activity.

The legal presumption serves to shift the burden of proof from the taxpayer to the Government.

This page left intentionally blank.

GENERAL SUSPENSE AND
IRC SECTION 183(e) PROCEDURES

The taxpayer may elect to postpone a determination of whether or not an activity is engaged in for profit. An individual taxpayer, S Corporation, trust or estate can make the election. This election is initiated by the taxpayer. The postponement moves the determination to the end of the fourth taxable year for cattle operations and to the end of the sixth taxable year for horse breeding activities following the year when the taxpayer first engages in a particular activity. In other words, the maximum postponement period is five years from the year of inception for most activities and seven years in the case of horse breeding, training, showing, or racing.

The election must be filed no later than the earlier of:

• Three years after initial statutory due date of the activity's first year's return, or;
• Sixty days after the taxpayer receives a written notice from a District Director that proposes to disallow the deduction attributable to that activity because the activity is not for profit.

IRC SECTION 183(e) SUSPENSE CASES

IRC section 183(e) and Treas. Reg. section 12.9 sets forth guidelines for the taxpayer's election to postpone a determination with respect to the presumption described in IRC section 183(d).

Form 5213 will be included in the case file. A copy of the form will be included in the file when received by the examiner or the taxpayer will submit the original during the examination.

If the taxpayer has not already submitted a Form 5213, the examiner should inform the taxpayer of IRC section 183(e) provisions if the Statute of Limitations has not expired for the activity's first return.

The examiner should verify that the Form 5213 has been timely filed.

The examiner needs to refer to local District procedures for further information regarding case processing and closing under IRC section 183(e) provisions.

This page left intentionally blank.

INITIAL INTERVIEW

RELATED TO CATTLE AND HORSE ACTIVITIES

1. Describe the activity engaged in on the Schedule.

2. What is your (taxpayer's) background in the activity? (Include # years, any formal training, practical experience)

3. Do you have others (employees, trainers, consultants, etc.) involved in the activity? (Include names)

4. On what criteria were the other individuals selected and by whom? (Detail any professional credentials)

5. What is the level of experience and expertise of these individuals? (Include # years, formal training, practical experience)

6. With respect to the activity, how much time do you devote on a daily basis? Weekly basis?

7. How much time is devoted by any other individuals on a daily basis? Weekly basis?

8. How much direction do the other individuals receive with respect to their expected performance of their duties?

9. What is the actual authority of these individuals?

10. What is the perceived authority of these individuals? (In other words, what authority would third parties perceive these individuals to have?)

11. To what level do these individuals exercise their own judgment with respect to their duties?

12. How did the activity get started?

13. How long has the taxpayer engaged in the activity?

14. How was the activity financed? (gift, inheritance, loan, or cash)

15. Why was this activity selected for venture? Describe any investigation.

16. What has made the activity to be historically unprofitable? Provide specific dates and describe any unforeseen circumstances.

17. What specific measures and changes have been implemented to reduce costs and increase profitability.

18. Are any assets expected to increase in value? List specific assets.

19. What is the basis for any expectation for increased value of certain assets? (Has taxpayer provided any written real estate comparables?)

20. Describe the success of other ventures or the lack thereof.

21. How many acres are involved with this activity? (Distinguish between owned and leased)

22. From whom is any acreage leased?

23. How is the acreage being utilized?

24. How many animals are using this acreage? (Calculate number and type of animal per acre)

25. What type of grass is present in the pastures?

26. Describe any pasture improvements. (Include any fertilizers, pesticides, herbicides, mowing, excavation, installation of any ponds or other watering reservoirs)
-

27. Was anyone consulted regarding these improvement decisions? (Include specific names)

28. Who completed these improvements? For how much?

29. Why were these improvements implemented?

30. Describe any plans for future improvements.

31. How will these improvements be financed?

32. How is the acreage partitioned into pastures and what is the significance and use of these pastures?

33. How are the pastures used and rotated (if rotated)?

34. Are you growing any crops for feed to the livestock? (list specific items such as hay or grain)

35. Have you purchased any hay or feed when your own hay or grain was depleted?

36. Describe any custom hire (machine or labor).

37. List any other hired workers. Were any Forms 1099 required to be filed?

LIVESTOCK BREEDING PROGRAM:

38. What type of livestock is being raised? How many?

39. Who selects the animals for the breeding program?

40. What criteria are used for this selection?

41. What type of animal are you breeding for?

42. Is this a registered herd with a recognized breed association? Name the breed association.

43. How long have you been a member of the breed association?

44. How many animals are registered annually?

45. What criteria are used to select animals for culling?

46. If not a registered herd but a commercial herd, what breed(s) are used in the program?

47. How many breeding females are in the program?

48. How many breeding males are in the program?

49. Do you own the studs or do you use artificial insemination?

50. How do you select the sires for the program?

51. What kind of maintenance program do you use for the breeding males?

52. How many breeding males are exposed to the females at any one time? (Examiner note: Only one male should be with the females at any one time in order to maintain accurate performance and breeding records).

53. Do you use artificial insemination?

54. Who performs the artificial insemination?

55. Describe the method of recordkeeping that is in place for the breeding program.

56. Does this recordkeeping system track the live births, birth weights, weaning weights, service sires?

57. At what age are the offspring weaned? Describe the weaning process.

58. How are the offspring disposed? Are any used for replacements in the herd? Sold as feeders? Sold as registered stock?

59. Are any of the animals showed at any livestock shows and competitions? Frequency?

60. How are the showing expenses treated within the books and records as well as the tax return?

61. What awards and honors have been received with respect to the showing?

COMMERCIAL BREEDING PROGRAM:

62. What breeds are used within the herd? Why?

63. Describe the feeding program? (Include percentage of protein, any supplements, so forth)

64. Are there any records which track weaning weights, daily rate-of-gain for the feedlot animals?

65. When are the animals weighed?

66. At what age or weight are the animals sold?

67. How many animals are sold annually?

68. Are any females retained as replacements in the herd?

69. Are any animals purchased for resale? How many? How long are those animals kept prior to resale? Describe any feeding program utilized prior to sale?

70. Describe the type of animal being selected for purchase and subsequent resale (include weights at time of purchase and weights at time of resale, as well as approximate ages at time of purchase and subsequent resale).

71. Who makes the selection of these animals and why?

72. Who determines when the animals are ready to sell?

USE OF ANY EXPERTS OR ADVISORS:
73. Have you relied upon any experts or advisors?

74. Cite instances where you have chosen to implement your advisor's recommendations?

75. How did the advisor's recommendations impact the performance of the activity?

76. Describe any instances when you have chosen not to heed the advice of the expert and state why?

OTHER RELATED QUESTIONS:
77. Have you received any agricultural subsidies during any periods that the activity is in operation?

BUSINESS PLAN:
78. Do you have a written business plan?

79. How was this business plan prepared?

80. When was this business plan formalized into writing? (At the commencement of the activity or for the purpose of the examination?)

81. Who assisted with the preparation of the business plan?

82. Who was consulted during the investigation of the activity prior to the commencement of the activity?

83. What real estate comparables were acquired prior to the commencement of the activity?

84. Does the business plan cover all years of the activity's history as well as forecasting into future years?

85. Does the business plan allow for any contingencies due to unforeseen circumstances?

86. How does the business plan determine gross receipts for each year?

87. Is the gross receipts computation reasonable?

88. How were the expenses determined or estimated for use in the forecast?

89. What justifies the reasonableness of the forecasted expenses?

90. Show how the business plan presents any semblance of an economic forecast for the activity?

91. During what specific year does the economic forecast show the activity turn around and become profitable?

92. What events and circumstances will cause the activity to be profitable in that particular tax year?

93. (If the business plan does not present any form of an economic forecast), when do you foresee the activity becoming profitable? (Designate a specific year).

94. What specific events will have occurred to enable this turnaround?

95. Why have you not abandoned the activity in light of the history of losses?

96. If this activity should never be likely to generate a net profit, would you abandon the activity?

97. What aspects of personal pleasure or recreation do you, or other related individuals, derive from the activity?

TAX SAVINGS BENEFIT ANALYSIS *

Tax Period	Tax with Loss	Tax without Loss	Tax Savings
1985			
1986			
1987			
1988			
1989			
1990			
1991			
1992			
1993			
1994			
1995			
1996			
1997			
TOTALS			

* This analysis may also be applicable with respect to Property Tax Savings when a taxpayer has derived such a tax benefit due to agricultural status. This benefit is also known as an agricultural exemption.

This page left intentionally blank.

Glossary of Terms

PURPOSE

This list of market segment-specific terminology is frequently used in conjunction with horse and cattle. These definitions may assist the examiner. Any slang and regional terminology will be further defined.

Amateur: A person who has not shown, trained, judged, or assisted in training a horse for remuneration. Eligibility requirements may vary among the governing associations. Similar to Non-Pro status.

Artificial Insemination (AI): Medical process by which semen has been collected from a stud (bull or horse) and is used to impregnate a breeding female (cow or mare). Usually performed by a veterinarian or specially trained professional. This is a more costly method for breeding than the natural method (live cover). Stud owners must supply breeding certificates to the owners of the females so that the offspring may be registered with the breed association. At the time of this writing, Thoroughbred horses may not be bred through AI.

Bull: A breeding male for cattle.

Calf: Any offspring from a bovine or cow.

Carrying capacity: Measurement tool that recommends the number of adult animals that may be supported per acre of land. Varies among regions. Determined by the annual rainfall and amount of grass produced for grazing per acre. To exceed the recommended carrying capacity results in reduced grazing supply and increases the need for supplemental feed.

Colt: A young male horse.

Cow: A breeding female for cattle.

Cow horse: Any horse that has bloodlines strong in the parentage of horses that work heavily with cattle. Especially cutting, roping, and team penning horses. A horse may be described as "cowy" if that horse possesses a lot of "cow sense". That horse has the ability to anticipate the movement of the cow and generally works well with cattle.

Day care: Care provided for horses that are traveling on the show circuit.

Embryo Transfer (ET): Program by which a donor cow has her fertilized embryos flushed from her body and transferred to the uterus of a recipient cow (recip). The recip will give birth to the calf and raise the calf. This process enables beef cattlemen to replicate their best quality females and produce multiple calves from these top females annually. In other words, one cow could produce multiple calves annually.

Farrier: Professional who puts horseshoes on horses.

Filly: A young female horse who has not been bred and had a foal.

Finals: A round of competition that generally determines a winner and placings.

Flush: Term used with Embryo Transfer (ET). Medical process by which fertilized embryos are removed from the donor cow. Usually performed by a veterinarian or other specially trained professional.

Foal: Any offspring from a horse.

Gelding: A neutered male horse.

Go-round: A preliminary round of competition that determines competition finalists.

Halter-bred horse: Any horse that has bloodlines strong in the parentage of horses that compete primarily in halter classes. Some Halter Horses are never broke to ride.

Halter horse: Any horse that competes in halter classes.

Halter class: Competition in which the conformation of the horse is judged. The horses are shown without a rider. The exhibitor stands at the side of the horse.

Heifer: A young female bovine that has never had a calf.

Incentive fund: Special multimillion dollar awards program sponsored by the American Quarter Horse Association (AQHA) by which eligible horse owners and breeders may earn monies based upon points earned in AQHA open and amateur competitions. Refer to the sponsoring association for specific rules and guidelines. Horse enrollment is required for participation.

Jackpot: Money paid by exhibitors or competitors in addition to the entry fees. This money is kept separate from the entry fees and distributed among the top finishers.

January 1: The birthday used by governing associations of any horse regardless of the true birthdate. For example, a foal born on December 31, 1998, becomes one year old on January 1, 1999. For depreciation purposes, the actual birthdate of the foal determines the age.

Live cover: Process by which natural methods are used to breed a female, as opposed to Artificial Insemination (AI).

Mare: A female horse who has been bred or has had a foal.

Mare care: Care provided for mares. May include breeding services (artificial insemination), prenatal care, postnatal care, and foal care. Generally provided at a breeding facility.

Non-Pro: A person who has not attained Professional status per criteria of the governing association. Refer to the governing association for status requirements. In general, this status is based upon money earned in competition to date.

Open: a) A competition that does not have exhibitor age or experience restrictions to enter.
b) A breeding female that is not bred.

Paint horse: A horse that has too much white hair to be registered as an American Quarter Horse.

Performance class: An event where either the horse or the rider is judged upon their actions. Examples include reining and cutting horse competitions.

Performance horse: Any horse that participates in an event such as cutting, roping, barrel racing, pole bending, reining, or team penning. These horses may also be referenced by their respective specialty event, such as a cutting horse or a roping horse. While the horse should have some natural talent and ability for such events, training is still required to develop these horses.

Points: Awarded to qualifying horses through show competitions sanctioned by the governing association.

Professional (Pro): A person who has exceeded the money earnings cap as a Non-Pro competitor. Refer to the governing association for eligibility requirements.

Quarter Horse: Another name for the American Quarter Horse breed.

Recipient cow (recip): Cow who receives an implanted embryo from a donor cow, carries the embryo to birth, and subsequently raises the calf as her own. Used in Embryo Transfer (ET) programs. Beef cattlemen have frequently used dairy cows as recipient cows.

Replacement heifer: Heifer who has been designated to join a breeding herd program. Frequently has been an offspring from the herd for which she has been designated to join as a breeding cow.

Speed event: A class that is judged solely by a timer.

Speed Index (SI): A method by which horses are rated by their speed abilities. Usually computed for performance horses and racehorses.

Stallion: A breeding male horse.

Standing fee: A fee derived for the breeding services of a stud horse. May come with a guarantee for live offspring (Live Foal Guarantee – LFG). May be a source of revenue for the stud owner or an expense for the mare owner.

Steer: A neutered male bovine. Raised for beef production.

Stud: A breeding male. May be used to refer to cattle or horses.

Tack: Includes the saddle, bridle, headstalls, reins, blankets, pads, bits, and other equipment used to prepare the horse for use by the rider. A common component on Depreciation schedules.